DEEP CONVICTION

More Life Lessons From My Time Behind Bars

Shane Flemens

DEEP CONVICTION
Copyright © 2020 by Shane Flemens

DEDICATION

Dedicated to the late Lorn Harris, Lloyd Mervin Brett, and Elsie Rose Johnson.

It is only when you realize that life is taking you nowhere that it begins to have meaning.

-Shane Flemens

In 2008, Shane Flemens was convicted of assault in the first degree in Kodiak, Alaska. He was sentenced to nineteen years in prison, with nine years suspended. He spent nearly a decade in correctional facilities in Alaska and Colorado.

In prison, Shane worked hard to do the things he was ordered to do by the judge and to go along with the system. This book, the follow-up to his first book, CONVICTION, contains even more stories from his time inside and the lessons he hopes will wake up at least one person to the unimaginable realities of prison life in the hopes they will avoid his experiences and losses. This book also explores the intractable dysfunction and pressing crisis of the industrial prison complex of the United States.

All names used in the book have been changed to protect their identity, unless explicitly noted.

TABLE OF CONTENTS

INTRODUCTION 9

CONSEQUENCES IN KODIAK 11

KODIAK-GETTING TO WORK 18

LOCKDOWN 28

LOWEST COMMON DENOMINATOR 35

KODIAK-GETTING INTO TROUBLE 39

MY JOBS PLAN 43

CAN I IN KENAI? YES, I CAN! 47

INNER WORKINGS OF A BROKEN SYSTEM 54

THE COMPANY YOU KEEP 60

MY BROTHER'S BROTHER 64

ALPHA MALES 71

TROUBLE IN ALPHA 75

LAST HAIRCUT...EVER? 78

MATT 81

THE VETERAN 84

CAMERON 90

PAUL 92

ADAM 94

SECOND SHOT AT ALPHA 98

CLASSIFICATION 102

CERTIFICATE 107

THERE HAS TO BE A BETTER WAY 110

AFTERWORD 114

ABOUT THE AUTHOR 115

INTRODUCTION

In my first book, CONVICTION, I introduced you to parts of my life's journey from the serious crime I committed to some of the painful consequences that resulted.

I have been humbled by, and feel so grateful for, the warm and caring reception from so many people who read my book and shared how my lessons have benefitted them personally, or someone they love. I have been able to share my message of conviction and second chances more broadly than I ever thought possible and I am hopeful that this second book will reach even more people and affect positive change in whatever way I can. *This* is why I have written these books: **to help people change**. And the hard work I put in during my incarceration, and since then, compels me to share the love and valuable lessons I gained.

Also, having directly seen and personally experienced the inner workings of the prison system I believe I have a moral obligation to share my perspectives with the outside world. In so doing I aim to raise awareness of the dysfunction of the system as the first step to affecting change for the 2,300,000 inmates still inside and suffering within it. If we are to ever help actually rehabilitate our fellow Americans and improve the overall good of our society the need for change is urgent and deep.

In this book, I have included questions at the end of some of the chapters for YOU, the reader, to carefully consider. My view is that the "correctional" system in the United States isn't actually correcting anyone. In fact, the system itself needs to be corrected. We can and must do better.

Nelson Mandela, another man who spent many years in prison said something that cuts to the core:

"It is said that no one truly knows a nation until one has been inside its jails. A nation should not be judged by how it treats its highest citizens, but its lowest ones."

Thank you for reading about my experiences in prison. I look forward to hearing from you and welcome your participation in the change we all need.

To learn more or get in touch please visit http://shaneflemens.com or email us at team@shaneflemens.com.

Thank you and may God bless you.

CONSEQUENCES IN KODIAK

It's early summer of 2009 and I'm getting ready for sentencing. For the 6th or 7th time in the year since my arrest, I'm transferring back from the holding facility in Anchorage one last time to Kodiak for my court appearance. Just like every time, I am in handcuffs and waist restraints. It's humiliating. On the bright side, I do get some fresh air which is a welcome change from the stagnant, heavy air inside the prison walls. The transport van pulls up to the curb at the Anchorage airport and I notice a nice-looking woman just barely walking through the front doors. I can't see her face but there is something familiar about her.

It crosses my mind that it might be my sister, Rachel Ammerman. She and her husband were coming in to town for my sentencing and they were connecting through Anchorage since there aren't really any direct flights into Kodiak from the Lower 48.

The van stops and the officer transporting me to Kodiak gets me out and I briefly step into the beautiful, clean Alaskan air. We walk into the airport and my eyes find the woman I saw outside and it *is* my sister. I have not seen anyone that I know for a year now. I started to cry, but held back since people were around and I obviously had already drawn a lot of attention with the handcuffs and police escort. The officer wasn't thrilled with this totally unplanned reunion but mercifully allowed us to visit. It was

11

something I will never forget. Before we knew it, my flight is leaving and we have to head to the gate. I give my sister a huge hug. My brother-in-law actually wanted one, too, and that touched me.

We get to Kodiak finally and I am put into a cell with everyone else. I had been here so many times this year that I pretty much know everyone in there. Or, I should say, they knew me or had at least heard about me. Many of them also knew the victims of my crime. Apparently rumors about the incident were flying and lots of things were being said. Even though I had pled guilty for my actions in the incident it wasn't that cut and dried. I'm not sure if many crimes really are. But, regardless of what was being said, and what rumors were circulating here is what I knew was true the day this all started:

- The incident occurred while we were way out in the ocean. The one crewmate was really hurt and needed immediate medical attention. The water was rough so when the Coast Guard helicopter was ready to lift him in the basket, I helped secure the line to keep it as steady as we could.

- After he was secured in the chopper, the less injured crewmate (withholding his name for privacy reasons) turned to me and asked me to not say anything about the drugs. He pointed out that if I did report it the skipper would face serious consequences and possibly lose the boat. I told him

I wouldn't say anything. We hugged and went our separate ways; him to the hospital and me to jail.

- Later, the blood work of my two stabbed crewmates both showed evidence of illegal drugs in their system. (I have no idea how this information wasn't used to get the skipper or the victims in trouble but it didn't change what I did and I kept my word.)

- The results of my cheek swab and breathalyzer were clean.

During this 24-hour period I am awaiting the sentencing in the jail there in Kodiak, I actually meet the brother-in-law of one of my former crewmates from the boat. He was in general holding for a crime he had committed. (Yeah, the fishing business in Alaska is rough.) He tells me I have no chance of getting a light sentence. When I ask why, he tells me the judge and my crewmates' fathers are close friends. My stomach jumped into my throat. I alerted my attorney to this and he simply replied with something like, "It's fine. Things like this happen here."

Further, I was informed that this same crewmate who was, of course, testifying against me was also about to sue the skipper. After he had recovered from his injuries, he got the skipper to re-hire him but was apparently was actually using the job to be close to him for any helpful information as he launched his lawsuit alleging negligence

13

for the incident when I stabbed him. It was shocking and frustrating to know this man was lying to the skipper.

I had no choice. No say. I just had to sit back and watch all this go down.

Court isn't until tomorrow, and other than listening to the scuttlebutt in the jail there wasn't much to do. Thankfully, my sister came to see me and we got to spend a couple hours chatting while she and her husband were there.

When we get to court the next day, I could tell something wasn't right. My lawyer had assured me all the motions had been addressed and the paperwork was in order. This sentencing had been on the docket for months now. I lean forward to listen as best I can but barely make out anything more than the lawyers and judge saying my hearing is postponed for a week.

My family had flown all the way to Kodiak to be there for my sentencing and after all of that effort and expense they are ultimately unable to attend my sentencing because they had to get back to jobs and family and couldn't wait another week. So, my family leaves. And I get put back into my cell where I will wait another week to learn my fate. After an entire year of proceedings, the Court suddenly postpones the sentencing for a week and my family can't attend. I find that just too strange to be a coincidence.

14

This wasn't the first time I had some issues with my attorney and the court proceedings. Over the one-year period of incarceration since my arrest, I had been seen by several doctors, psychiatrists, and counselors. One of the leading doctors in the State had given me a clean bill of mental health. I told her I already knew I was mentally healthy, more or less, and she just looked at me and walked off.

I called my attorney right then to let him know what the psychiatrist said. He was concerned that not having a diagnosed mental health issue would have a negative impact on my sentencing and encouraged me to be less than forthright about it. (Remember, like it or not, a defense attorney's sole job is to get their client, me in this case, out of trouble and lighten whatever kind of punishment the judge hands out.) The truth is that the intense anxiety I was feeling felt to me like a bona fide mental health issue.

However, I have never had a diagnosed chronic mental health issue in my life and I couldn't lie about it. That said, I had done plenty of partying and drug use and, while it was unclear exactly what happened to me that day on the boat, I fear that I may have had a really ill-timed bout of episodic paranoia related to my drug use. So, I went along with his advice, more or less.

Otherwise, my mental health and physical health in general have always been good. But given the nature of the crime I committed I was sometimes put in mods, or sections of the prison, with guys who *did* have diagnosed mental health issues and I had the chance to see first-hand what that really looks like. Even though it was a bit unsettling, even scary at times, I cared about these guys, learned lots of information, and witnessed the way the system operated. I am grateful for these lessons but was always glad to be released from these mental health mods.

Anyway, the week in Kodiak goes by and the postponed hearing finally takes place. I am sentenced to nineteen years, with nine years suspended[1], for my conviction of first-degree assault. I just received ten years in prison.

Holy crap! That just happened!

The judge leaves me with some words of wisdom and a verbal slap in the face:

First, the wisdom: "If you listen to me and carefully follow my instructions you will leave prison a productive member of society. You will live a normal life. But only if you listen to me."

He issued his orders for me that day. I followed them to a T.

Then, the slap in the face: "I'm making an example out of you. You are an outsider in Alaska."

---

[1] The judge could have made me do all nineteen years but only made me serve ten.

He gave me 10 years in prison.

Kodiak, Alaska may be where I very painfully lost my freedom, but it's also where I found it 13 years earlier.

KODIAK-GETTING TO WORK

I had just turned 21 that first summer I spent in Alaska. A friend I had met in my hometown of Wenatchee, Washington, let's call him Peru, knew how much I absolutely loved fishing. He tells me all he knows about Alaska and the allure of it, especially for a young man who had never really left home, was just too much to not go.

The truth is I have no idea what I'm getting myself into. The trip was equal parts amazing and scary. As most good coming-of-age adventures begin, Peru gets us a "40 sack" of marijuana for our travels. It's only $40 worth of weed but it stinks. We get to the airport and he hands me the bag. I shrug my shoulders, think to myself, "It's just weed," and I put it in my sock. I walk through security like I owned it thinking since it's not that much, they would just take it if they find it. I breeze through the metal detector, grab my bags off the x-ray machine belt, and head off to the gate.

We board the plane and take off for the Last Frontier.

Our flight is the red-eye flight so we get to Anchorage at 4AM and it's already light outside. We are only connecting here on our way to Kodiak and have a bunch of time to kill so we walk a few blocks to crash at a cheap motel. There were birds flying all around me on the walk in the crisp morning air and I was in awe of Alaska

18

already. I'm thinking, "so far, so good" and am excited to be there.

That afternoon we head back to the airport to catch our small prop plane for Kodiak, our final destination. Let me tell you, if I would've known this plane ride was going to be so rough, I definitely would've taken the ferry. The takeoff is really bumpy. The entire flight is over water and the turbulence doesn't stop. Thankfully, we start to descend but it gets even rougher. We get closer and closer to what should be the ground but all I see is water.

I'm grabbing my seat more tightly now and, finally, rocks appear below and we hit the runway fast. The pilot hits the brakes, hard, and my head lurches forward as we come to almost a complete stop in just seconds. Turns out the runway is not very long and I just learned that the hard way. And with that unsettling landing, I am in Kodiak, Alaska, happily clueless about what's in store for me on this trip, or the future one that will change my life forever.

We get our bags, hop in a cab and hit downtown Kodiak. I have a total of $500 to my name and Peru and I split a motel. Rooms are about a hundred bucks, which feels pretty expensive to me but this is when I learn that everything in Alaska is two to three times more expensive than the lower 48. I realize that my $500 is going to go fast. I need a fishing job but don't know how to find one.

We get to our room, drop our bags, and smoke a bowl to calm ourselves after our horrific flight. Frayed nerves now a little less frayed, we head out the door to go find work. I have *zero* idea what I am doing and remind myself that Peru talked me into this. We hit the docks nearby and there are rows and rows of countless fishing boats. I see the Saga, the Cornila Marie, and other boats that, in a few years, will be featured on the popular TV series, Deadliest Catch. Looking back, I realize that some of the guys I got to hang out with that summer would actually be on the show. Some of these guys were pretty ornery, and some were even a little crazy.

Back to my job hunt. So, it's the summer of 1996 and I find out that it's Salmon season. I'm digging this. I love fishing and it's nothing but fishing boats, like, everywhere. Despite this, I have no flippin' idea which boats fished for what, but my buddy, Peru, and I, still half-high, hit the docks. We decide to leave notes on boats called *seiners* (Salmon boats) letting them know we are available for hire and that we've come a long way to be there. We also let them know our motel and room number so they can find us.

After leaving a dozen or so notes and talking with a few skippers and their crew, we grab a sandwich at the local Subway and go back to the motel. We had just finished smoking our second bowl of the day when someone knocked on our door. Our room is still full of smoke from our illegal weed so we try, in vain, to cover it

20

up. More knocks at the door. It's too late and we know there's nothing we can do so we open the door. Two guys are standing there, both of them younger than Peru and I; they can't be older than 18. The taller one goes, "We smoke too, don't worry," he continues, "I'm Skip of the Calib salmon boat." He got our note.

Over another bowl we all proceed to talk about fishing and what we needed to do. They liked us and we were hired, just five hours after getting to Kodiak. But this job won't last long. We grab our things and head to the boat, a 38-foot seiner. We throw our bags on our bunks. Peru takes the bunk on the port side. The Skip takes us to the marine supply store to get us our gear. We get fishing licenses, rain gear, boots, gloves, and rubber bands to seal our rain gear around our wrists and ankles. We are all suited up and ready for the season, which is about to get under way.

We make a "practice set" (basically all the equipment involved in dropping and retrieving the nets to catch the fish.) Deploying and retrieving the "set" involves a hydraulic system and we fiddle around with a set of hydraulic hose brakes, fix a cracked hose, and head back to shore.

I very quickly realize that my 18-year-old skipper is a party machine, much more interested in partying than he is in fishing. This is a problem for me. Much as I liked to party back then, I'm in Alaska looking to make some real money, real fast. The season has started and we aren't fishing. As feared, my $500 is now down to $100 and without a change in circumstances it'll be $0 before too long.

So, Peru and I decide we gotta find a different boat and get to work. We head up to the pier where I first meet an aggressive monster of a sea lion, One Eye. One Eye is a "local" and the rumors had it that he had once dragged a fisherman to the bottom of the harbor because the fisherman threw him a salmon with a beer bottle stuffed inside. This pissed off One Eye I guess, and he made this fisherman pay for it.

Anyways, we get up to the dock on the pier and see two dirty, old fishermen headed towards us. They looked and smelled as you would imagine: in desperate need of showers, foul-smelling filthy clothes, faces that hadn't seen the good side of a razor in a very long while. Picture dirty road crew workers after a long day, except on the water, in the last frontier. They say they needed a guy to go "dragging."[2] We both knew dragging was big money. Some people hated draggers because it's a crude method of fishing, one in which you just drag the ocean floor and catch whatever is in the way of the nets. But you could make thousands in just days and that sounded great

Peru looks at me and says, "I'll do it."

---

[2] https://en.wikipedia.org/wiki/Bottom_trawling

I realize in that instant that I am about to be on my own. He takes the weed that's left, it's his anyways, they go to the boat, the guys help him with his things, and he was gone. I didn't think I would ever see him again but I was happy for him.

I, on the other hand, was a little sad and a little scared. I was alone now, with almost no money and "working" for a skipper that was partying every night. Reflecting on this time now, I think this actually helped me get through all my alone time in prison. God was just building me up to that. I talked myself into looking for a different job.

So, I get up the next day and hit the docks looking for work. I go to a coffee shop to get an Italian soda. I talk with the girl at the counter and, luckily, she seemed to like me. I tell her I', looking for a job and we visit for a bit. She takes my name and the name of the boat I'm on. A few hours later, a nice, young couple walk towards my boat, holding hands and ask me my name. "Shane," I tell them. Turns out they are indeed a very nice Christian couple and they offered me a job on the spot.

I gratefully, and quickly, accepted their offer. But I told them, "I didn't want to just abandon the other skipper, so could we leave tomorrow?" They agreed and said, "We'll see you at 10AM to help with your things. So, (almost) just like that my career as a fisherman was launched.

That night, over beers with some locals, I told my first skip I had found another job. He wasn't too broken up over this news and I'm not too sure he even paid much attention to what I had said. Nonetheless, I woke up in the morning, packed my things, and, sure enough, my new skipper was there to help me load my things into his truck. We had to drive across the bridge to Dog-Bay, to get to the boat. Years later his small fleet would be on Harbor Side, which was much more in the center of the action.

The next day I become an official crewmember on the Wildgoose, and *my* salmon season finally starts. I make $3,000 in four days! I am, of course, relieved to have some money back in my pockets and feel lucky that I am also on a boat where praying at mealtime is the norm. I really enjoyed the prayers. My Grandma taught me the power of praying. However, at this point I was not yet ready to change my life and fully embrace God. I realize now that He had quite a few more lessons I needed to learn.

We delivered our first load of fish to the tender[3]. A tender is a much larger boat with the capacity to receive our load of fish and transport it to the plants where the fish is processed. This is when I meet the first guy I will see on the TV series Deadliest Catch years down the road. He was cool and we hit it off. We even hung out in town a few

---

[3] https://www.theakshow.com/post/how-to-be-a-salmon-tenderman-in-alaska

times. As a matter of fact, I'm watching Deadliest Catch years later and recognize him as the guy who throws a life ring in the ocean to save a guy.

I find out firsthand that fishing is indeed one of the deadliest jobs you can do, and it's not just the unforgiving, massive power of the ocean you have to watch out for. I also find out that Alaska is the number one state for disappearances in the USA[4]. In the vast wilderness that is Alaska there are numerous reasons people disappear and even more why they are never found. And when you combine some of the rowdiest men on the planet, perhaps escaping something in the Lower 48, with the wads of cash many of them just carry around with them you start to understand why. One of the quickest ways to a quickly double your money is to be there to take the wad of cash off somebody who suddenly "disappears," right?

I thank God to this day that I was lucky enough to get on a boat that prays before meals. Given the stories I have heard of violence out here in the midst of a very unforgiving ocean, I am always grateful that I had a skipper that was a careful, good man. I still pray for the fleet today. I've been fishing now for about a month. I love my job. It's pretty easy and I'm seeing some of the most beautiful scenery I've ever seen. The air is out of this world; clean and crisp. I am surrounded by whales and dolphins. And, somehow, I'm always running into old One Eye. I'm sure he remembers me. I sure remember him.

---

[4] https://www.latimes.com/archives/la-xpm-2005-feb-15-na-vanished15-story.html

I'm also making tons of money. I'm still thinking about Peru, though. I liked him. Despite being a greenhorn I'm now the "lead man[5]" on the boat. The "lead" refers to the heavy lead-filled line that sinks the net to the bottom and the lead man's main job is to stack the net on deck after it's brought up. I can also do most of the other jobs on the boat and I love it all! I am sure there is a connection between liking the job and doing it well.

One day I had an experience that taught me how quickly this job can remind you of Who is in charge. We were bringing the "purse bag[6]" onto the boat on a really rough weather day. The winds were blowing fiercely, about 40 knots, and I am doing my thing as the lead man, stacking the nets and the wind almost blows me into the net. (This is nothing compared to what I'll experience later in my career, however, I thought I was in a flippin' hurricane.)

One of the downsides of this job is that, in addition to the fish we are trying to catch, the nets also catch jellyfish, lots of them, as they skim the surface of the water as we bring them in. Well, as lead man, you are directly exposed to these little buggers. Usually you can avoid the sting of the jellyfish by keeping exposed skin away from the nets but when you fall into them because of the wind or whatever, you will be stung. And I was!

---

[5] https://saltwatersoldiers.net/2013/04/19/commercial-fishing-photo-of-the-day-the-lead-man/
[6] Nets full of fish.

26

My face is on fire, and my eyes almost swollen shut. The red jellyfish hurt the worse. It's like instantly getting a severe sunburn every time a tentacle touches your face. One or two might not be so bad but literally dozens touch my face every set of nets we bring in. Ouch!! Within an hour the pain starts to stop, but then we "pull the pin" to bring in another net and the pain starts all over as I get hit with more jellyfish stingers right in my face.

We bring in about 10k pounds of "reds[7]" which equals somewhere between $500 to $1,000. Not bad for an hour of work but, kids, stay in school! This is a hard life for many reasons. I do still love my job; I'm fishing.

---

[7] Red salmon

LOCKDOWN

After my sentencing was handed down in Kodiak, I was put into the Spring Creek Correctional Center in, otherwise lovely, Seward, Alaska, a maximum-security prison. I hit the yard and in the first five minutes I saw a guy that I had met in Anchorage Jail the previous year. He said, "watch this," and pointed. I looked to where he was pointing and saw this scary-looking bald dude, weighed about 230 pounds, all tattooed up, in his early 30s, sneak up on a 60-year-old inmate and violently attack him. He knocked him out almost instantly and just kept hitting him.

I found out later that he had broken this guy's jaw and fractured his cheek bone. Everyone just kept walking, pretending like nothing happened. This older guy just laid there, knocked out cold, and bleeding all over. I swallowed hard and thought to myself, "I am in the Devils Lair, and I'm in deep crap."

The prison guards ordered everyone to their cells and locked the whole prison down. The guards hadn't seen the attack and didn't know who had committed the beating but they were gonna try and find out. So, the COs[8] start going cell by cell to check every inmate's knuckles. They made us strip down to check for any signs of being in a fight: swollen knuckles or marks on our bodies. Little did the COs know that the bald guy wore gloves and attacked from behind. The 60-year-old didn't see it coming or even

---

[8] Correctional Officers

know what had happened. He didn't have the chance to fight back, which probably wouldn't have helped anyway.

There were no marks on anyone…except for the old man, so the guy who did it never got caught.

The next day, after being locked down for 24 hours, I saw the guy I knew from the yard and talked to him some more. He told me that he was in for 300 years for raping and murdering a woman. Scary? Yes! But there are worse cases in here.

And, of course, I asked him about the beating that took place in the yard yesterday. He told me his cellmate (the bald guy) was also in for rape and some of the "lifers[9]" made him attack this old guy because he disrespected one of them simply by saying "no." Apparently, the lifer asked the old man for a bag of Top Ramen (worth like $0.50) and a candy bar ($0.60). That's it. You would think "no big deal," right? Just give it to him and move on with your day.

But this is not how things work in prison. If the old man would have said "yes" and given him the ramen and the candy bar, then the lifer would keep coming back asking for more and more stuff. This eventually turns into making him pay "rent." In other words, he would make you pay him for living in "his" house. You see, to a lifer, prison has become the last "home" he will ever know. And if you

---

[9] Guys sentenced for life, or longer, and never getting out of prison.

aren't a lifer then you are just a guest, and, therefore, subject to house rules, including paying "rent."

This poor old man basically had two options; he could have said "yes," but then he would have been considered someone you can get things from, or a "Punk." And he would have been treated like a Punk the remainder of his prison term…by everyone. Or, he could have said "no" and get his face beat in. And that's unfortunately what he chose and exactly what happened.

What would you do? Terrifying, huh?

I had just been sent to Anchorage from Seward. One day the four of us were watching America's Got Talent on the TV. I had been pretty depressed, and the medication I was taking was not working. Honestly, at that point I didn't care if I lived or died, because of what I had been through and what I was facing in prison. I still remember the intensity of the numbness and sadness I was feeling.

Unfortunately, that night a young inmate in his early twenties was feeling that same depression even more intensely than I was, believing he had nothing to live for, and hung himself in the shower with a sheet. The staff and paramedics tried to revive him with CPR and even used a defibrillator but he had been dead too long when they found him.

Of course, given the way I was feeling that very night, I had to ask myself, "Why did he do this?" I thought about the answer for many months and eventually realized that he must have thought:

Nobody cared;
His life had no meaning;
People looked down on him for being in prison;
What would these people say after his release?
Would anyone even care if he was dead?

All of these tragic thoughts must have been going through his head that day he hung himself. The sad truth is that most people in prison have these very same thoughts, often. I know that because I had them myself...until that day.

As I watched them try to revive his lifeless body, I realized that people do care. If only he could have been in my shoes watching them try to save another human being. The staff and paramedics, accustomed to the brutality of prison, worked hard to try and bring him back; fear and even panic on their faces, running around, bumping into each other. All that effort for that one person who thought that nobody cared.

And in the midst of all of this craziness and almost panic I was stunned to hear my cellie laughing. He said he had seen worse and had done worse to numerous people. I then realized that I was sharing a cell with a hardened killer. I felt sick and really scared.

After this upsetting incident they held a meeting for us inmates and even brought staff from other prisons to talk about what had happened and help us "process" it, I guess. Some inmates had to get on medications to manage the emotional trauma of this experience.

Yes, people do care even if they don't say it or show it all the time. We need to remember that and also be sure that we remember to show more care and concern for others.

A "mod" is basically a housing unit where inmates live. There are about sixty-four inmates in a mod. And here in Anchorage there are four mods in one section of the prison. And there are numerous housing units. So, you can imagine how many inmates there actually are in this prison. Too many!

In one of these mods in the Anchorage holding facility there was this guy that would hang his mattress over the ladder to the top bunk and that guy would punch that mattress like a punching bag for hours every day. He claimed to be a cage fighter and professional boxer. I am not sure if that was true but he sure practiced like one.

One day a new guy came into his mod on some drug charges and he was just sitting in the cell writing a letter to his wife letting her know how much prison time he had just received. For no reason at all, the mattress-as-a-punching-bag guy ran into his cell, locked the door behind him, and started wailing on him. The guy writing the letter hadn't even been in the mod twenty minutes! And he was a pretty big guy, too.

These two started slamming each other against the concrete walls and tearing the place apart. It was really loud. You could see blood all over both of them. They kept fighting until the COs sprayed them with pepper spray. They were both put in the hole for thirty days. I'm not sure who won the fight but the guy who started it had his front tooth knocked out. The other guy had two black eyes and a bloody nose. About two years later I saw the guy missing his front tooth and I asked him, "Why did you do it?" He told me he was bored and had nothing to do.

QUESTION:

How is it that our "correctional" system is not providing inmates with as many programs and activities as possible to minimize or eliminate the boredom and waste of time?

Think of your life and tell me that you are progressing and growing when you have nothing to do. You aren't, right? Works the same way in prison.

33

As a society we must demand better of our officials and prisons to keep inmates busy and engaged in productive work that will help prepare them for release and re-entry into the world.

LOWEST COMMON DENOMINATOR

Even though Seward is a maximum-security prison there is no death row here like there is in other states where they segregate the worst-of-the-worst into an even more secure or isolated section of the prison. That means that all the inmates convicted of the most violent crimes: murder, rape, etc. are housed in the same mods as everyone else. There are tons of murderers here and you are housed with them, with serial killers, and the hit men of Alaska and it is very scary.

That said, the prison tries to distribute risk and keep order by assigning each inmate to one of three risk levels: Max closed, Medium, and Minimum. Max closed inmates essentially have no privileges. Medium inmates have some, and Minimum level has the fewest restrictions.

They further categorize inmates into one of two categories: "predator" or "prey." Sometimes they will put you into a group and assess your behavior for a week or so to see which mod makes the most sense. Based on my assault conviction, which is a violent crime, I am put into the predator group and housed in what's called the Kilo Mod, the roughest mod in Seward.

It was here that I meet another inmate with a story that broke my heart. He and I had talked numerous times and I knew he was doing hard time for a murder he

35

committed when he was only 18. He was 48 when I met him and still in prison. Yes, 30 years in prison!

After doing 30 years he was up for parole but was denied. The parole board told him to come back in 10 more years. Even if he made parole then that would mean 40 years in prison only to get out at the age of 58!

This guy told me that he had been repeatedly raped during his time behind bars. Even though this man, a teenager actually at the time of his crime, was a murderer, prison had cut him down to the lowest common denominator. Prison is a place where guys just like him, scary and dangerous to the public, can be and are raped at anytime and anyplace. It doesn't matter who you are or how you got inside; everyone is vulnerable and at-risk.

Lots of things led up to my time in Seward. I run into the scary Mohawk guy again. I wrote about him in my first book about our ride together in the back of a state trooper car when he told me, "If I didn't have handcuffs on, Flemens, I'd crush your skull." Yeah, that guy.

Well, when we meet this time at Seward, I am running things inside. Mohawk guy was new and seemed scared but, despite the way our last chat went, I was nice to him. Turns out this guy had talked with my crewmates from the incident on the boat and apparently, they are starting to tell the truth about what actually happened that day. And it's definitely not like what the paper is reporting. And yet, here I am in the worst mod in Seward.

In this mod the lifers had set up a hit on a guy and almost killed him. There is blood on the ceiling, the walls, the floors, and the door. The staff put crime tape across the door while doing the investigation into the attack. We were locked down for a couple of days.

The guards come in, and do a sweep on all the lifers. Some of these guys are going to the hole for setting up a hit and almost killing someone. They just need to determine who exactly was involved. So, the guards follow the prison cameras in reverse order to find out who executed the hit.

Once they determined which guys it was, the guards started to head to their cells and they didn't see it coming. The guards come in and take these guys to the hole. I get called out to run the mod. I'm really a no one here and am just laying low with my crowd while I get to know everyone and try and keep things cool.

You may not be surprised to know that there is sort of an order here inside operated informally, but tightly, by the inmates. As I mentioned above, prison is the home for the lifers so they run the drugs, the "store[10]," cell phones, girls, and even some of the staff. Carefully involving the staff is how they bring things in from the outside to sell,

---

[10] Where inmates can buy food, etc. but it's only open for limited hours.

including the girls. But I was just an inmate following the other ants. I hadn't yet started to think about God at this time except when I would see writings about Him on many of the cold concrete walls as I walked from cell to cell on my way somewhere.

So, I'm now running the only store and I really don't know what I'm doing exactly. I'm getting money, selling food by "tripling up," or marking up the prices by 300%. I am also selling tobacco and weed. I'm sober though. I'm doing no drugs and my mind is starting to function clearly. I'm getting "papered up.[11]" I'm working on programs and slowly starting to learn.

I'm starting to help the weaker inmates. I have food which means I have a little power and I'm using it to help the guys that are getting out of the gangs. Some of these guys would come in with broken arms, black eyes, and fingers all mangled from getting beaten up for trying to leave the gang. Often these severe injuries would force them to stay in their mod and have to miss "chow." They would come see me in the store and tell me their stories. I felt inspired to help these guys and would sometimes give them food for free because I wanted to support them in the effort to change their lives by getting out of the gangs.

So, much happened in Seward and, honestly, I still get scared to this day remembering just how rough it was. My recovery started there but my journey is just beginning.

---

[11] Making money, which I am reinvesting in my store by buying more goods to sell.

KODIAK-GETTING INTO TROUBLE

In Alaska, off the water there's lots of trouble, too. I'm out one night at a club called Mecca in Kodiak. There seems to be more drag queens here than any other place on earth so guys have to be careful. I'm drinking and I have thousands of dollars to my name now. And, I miss my family and two kids dearly so am trying to pass the time with some fun and almost anything to keep my mind off the pain of being away from them. I walk outside and run into Peru, we "bro" hug and smile. He tells me that day we separated he went fishing on the dragger for a few days but they never paid him. Tough luck.

I was thinking to myself, "that could've been me." God was looking after me, I just didn't know. Peru had no money and no job. I gave him a couple hundred bucks. We are hanging out and I'm still drinking. We go outside and he introduces me to a guy. This guy offends me right away with something he says and I head-butt him before he could say another word. I knocked him out and then went inside to get my coat. I had had enough for the night and was leaving.

I walk outside and he is still lying there. I turn around to head back to the boat when suddenly, out of nowhere, I'm tackled from behind. Somehow, I end up on top and see it's him. Apparently, he was conscious now. I raised my fist to hit him in the mouth but all of a sudden, I can't see. I'm like, "what just happened?!" My eyes are

39

burning and I can barely see. I then realize I had been maced…by a cop. This calms me down a little so I start to get off the guy. He tries to kick me but misses. I leave it alone.

Luckily, I had both of my crewmates with me. I gave them my wallet so they could bail me out of the jail I was about to be thrown in. That fight cost me $500 in bail money. Actually, I was arrested again years later for this incident in Dutch Harbor after King Crab season. See, I didn't stick around to attend the hearings of the charges against me for my role in this incident. Why? I was 21. The season was over and I just wanted to get home to my family. And basically, I didn't care.

Well, the judge cared and issued a bench warrant for my arrest which was still outstanding when the Coast Guard boarded our boat in Dutch Harbor for something totally unrelated. They discovered I had a warrant and arrested me on the spot. The lesson? Take care of your messes even when you don't want to. I promise you those messes will catch up to you and can make your life even harder than just taking care of them when they happen.

All things considered; I had a blast that summer. I, learned how to run a fishing boat. Met some great people; highlighted by my wonderful "adopted" Christian family that owned the Wildgoose. I learned a lot from them. Things that I didn't quite understand yet but that would lay a solid foundation that would serve me well over the next two decades in the growth of my faith.

I was off the boat again for a couple of days and wanted to blow off some steam. So, I rented a motel room and threw a party. Not that I needed an excuse to party but we had just lost a crew member from the team. One day he just decided to not show back up. This happens a lot in the fishing business. Guys just sort of move on without saying much. This was a bummer to me because I really liked this guy. God bless, Buck!

We had already hired at new guy to replace him. I'm drinking, which is not a good thing and I had a $500 draw[12] burning a hole in my pocket.

There are lots of girls in Alaska and at my party I meet one in a very interesting way. I will stay close to her for years. She was actually with the new guy we just hired but seemed to like me. Well, the new guy says something bad about my mom earlier in the evening and it's eating at me the more the night went on. I should have left it alone. I was doing really well for myself and life was pretty good. I was making tens of thousands of dollars and there were plenty of girls to choose from. Not bad for a 21-year-old!

The night goes on and as I was sitting on the dresser in the room, he walks right by me. I am bugged and can't

---

[12] Pay Advance

resist so I put my foot out and trip him. He pushes me and it was on. I beat the guy through the room, until he is all the way out in the hallway. Then he starts making strange noises and starts banging his own head into the motel wall.

This kinda freaked me out so I got out of there fast. I took a cab and a few miles down the road the cops catch up to me. Someone gave the cops a description of me and they found me. I was put in handcuffs and brought back to the motel. I was unaware he had banged his own head so much that he actually made a hole in the wall. The cop asked me if I had done it. I just looked at him and said nothing. I was still really pissed that this guy had said that about my mom. The hotel security dude steps in, answering for me, and tells the cops that it wasn't me that had caused the damage. So, they release me and go off to find the guy that did make the hole in the wall.

I get back to my room and the girl he was with was still there. I hang out with everyone all night, but especially her. I get her number and we stay in contact for years. We even go out on her dad's huge boat and made some great fishing stories together. I made $24,000 that summer and, needless to say, I was "hooked" on fishing in Alaska. The girls were wild, the bars never closed, and I was making thousands of dollars for just a few days of work. I loved fishing, the air was clean and made me feel more alive than I ever had. What else could I possibly ask for?!

MY JOBS PLAN

In the first year since my arrest, while all the court proceedings are happening, I'm being transferred back and forth from Kodiak to Anchorage frequently. I'm always putting a work "cop-out[13]" in for jobs. However, I had to learn that there are over a thousand inmates ahead of me wanting jobs as well. Job assignments go in order. I never received a job at the Anchorage Complex, but I tried to get one each and every time. I did go to the law library often so I could look up the various statutes, policies, and procedures to help understand how rules were being broken. I realized that the system was hurting deep within but at that point it was hard to see just how deeply the dysfunction went.

During this time, I was in at least 10 different mods so I got to meet lots of guys that would play a key part in my rehabilitation and my status throughout my stay in prison. Moving from place to place is a huge set back to inmate rehabilitation. It hurts families as well because when you move, any progress you were making is jeopardized. This interruption could affect your release and how you perform *after* you are released. Also, the likelihood of recidivism[14] increases and the cost to taxpayers is high because what was spent to rehab didn't work and then the costs are repeated to try again.

---

[13] A cop-out, or Inmate Request to Staff, is how things get done in prison. To make an appointment, to get permission to do anything you must send a cop-out through the staff.
[14] Recidivism is the tendency of a convicted criminal to repeat or reoffend a crime after already receiving punishment or serving their sentence. Source: www.worldpopulationreview.com

If you've ever moved to a different city or state then you know that the disruption to daily life by having to get acclimated to a new environment and routine can cause setbacks...and that is on the outside!

And like on the outside, many moves involve a change in jobs. In prison, jobs provide inmates with a routine and something productive to do all day. Yeah, the pay is ridiculously low ($0.50/hour) but it can add up and getting something of value in exchange for working, even just two quarters an hour, is somewhat fulfilling.

So, when it comes to prison jobs, I really think that having some sort of basic system where an inmate who performs his job well and follows the rules can have a chance for a sort of promotion, just like in jobs outside of prison. You start at the bottom, work hard, and get a raise based on your job performance. And maybe provide incentives, like a pay raise, as you accomplish tasks given to you by your boss.

I think this positive incentive concept should be a part of prison reform. If I were in charge it would go something like this:

- You get arrested and sent to prison.
- You start at the maximum risk level.
- You start with one of the worst jobs: cleaning toilets.

- Then, if you work hard and comply with the rules then maybe you work your way up to something less unpleasant: like walking the warden's precious dog or washing his sportscar. (I'm joking about the dog and the car, but you get my point, right?)

You then could get "upgraded" to medium risk by working hard and never getting what's called a "write-up."

The write-up system is significant in Alaskan prisons. A write-up is pretty much what it sounds like. If an inmate breaks a rule or gets out of line a write-up is issued and put into their record. Just one write-up can impact your privileges inside and even whether you get parole or not. In Alaska they are so strict that staff can and do give you a write-up just for having an extra pair of socks. (In all my time locked-up in numerous facilities I never received a write-up, that I wasn't able to prove was bogus. A few times I came very close and I have to credit the grace of God for helping me avoid even one going on my record.)

Part of moving up from medium risk level to minimum risk level would also include the following requirements:

- Completing court-imposed classes.
- Doing well by helping others.
- Following the rules.

The prison staff all know that an effective way to motivate an inmate to make positive changes is to provide perks and incentives. Things like:

- More "out time."
- Family calls.
- Better jobs.
- Options for work release.
- More items from home.
- Lower restrictions generally.
- Basic tools for success.

By doing it this way the system is now working because the rewards of compliance are worth it to the inmate and he is motivated to get more rewards through continued compliance with the system.

The ideal is that inmates are then moved to minimum risk level where they can work on life skills, securing housing for when they're released, engaging the support of family. All of these things the judge tells you to do in the beginning at sentencing. And the inmate should be able to effectively work on these things now that they have earned their way through this incentive system and are prepared to tackle these critical steps.

Doesn't this seem like a very common-sense and manageable approach? If only I were running the joint!

CAN I IN KENAI? YES, I CAN!

In 2011, I am transferred to Wildwood Correctional Complex in Kenai for the first time. It's about three years into my sentence and this was like my 10th move so far. Little did I know there were many more transfers to come.

After arriving to Kenai, I keep doing all I can to make the most of my time, you know, make lemonade out of lemons. Here is a list of all the things I accomplished in a little less than a year there. I don't share this to brag, not at all. I share this to show you what is possible and, perhaps, how things ought to be if we are ever to have any hope in reducing recidivism and making the most of prison.

- Completed a six-month faith-based program called Alpha[15].
- Worked directly with other inmates to help them get their GED. Turns out we produced more GED graduates than they ever had in that amount of time.
- Worked as many as three jobs at a time.
- Was consistent in paying my child support.
- In partnership with the Salvation Army I led the first-of-its-kind holiday fundraiser for underprivileged kids in Kenai-I talk about that amazing event in my first book, CONVICTION.

---

[15] This program is available outside the prison system, too. https://alphausa.org/about

- Completed numerous (~20) programs such as: anger management, brain injury class, and White Bison[16], to name just a few.
- Took a college placement test so I could take college classes.

Please understand that in doing all of the above I was simply following the judge's orders like all inmates should be doing, right?

I will say that I am proud of the fact that during this time I was released from all mental health holds which, according to the mental health staff there, they had only seen happen less than a handful of times in many years. So, in other words I was really kicking butt and meeting the challenges in front of me. And I will say that, for me at least, there was a strong correlation between staying busy and working hard and successfully managing the extreme mental and emotional stress all inmates have to endure in prison.

At this point I still don't understand the Bible or know what I'm doing but I do know that I'm progressing rapidly and I'm sober. This time in Kenai really is a pivotal period in my time in prison and I am grateful that I chose to follow the instructions from the judge. Afterall, judges are generally in that position because of their hard work and I believe that more times than not their instructions are based in wisdom and, therefore, worth listening to.

---

[16] A sobriety program. https://whitebison.org/

However, the prison in Kenai is full to the max. There are so many inmates that we are sleeping on the floor. As is my way, I keep talking to lots of inmates and listen to their stories.

One of my cellies is named Matt. We are cellies for a few months so I get to hear a lot of his stories, sometimes staying up all night listening to him talk about his crimes. I realize quickly that Matt is scary. Matt's dad had just passed away and foul play was suspected. (Later the suspicion is confirmed when I meet the guy who did it.)

One night, Matt tells me about the time he broke into a military armory and stole a case of grenades, a .50 caliber rifle, and thousands of tracer rounds. This crime was unknown until one night when Matt, in a drug-induced state, left a grenade under the mattress of a motel, which thankfully didn't go off, and the maid found it and reported it. The Feds were anxious to investigate stolen military-grade weapons.

Well, during this time while I'm continuing to work for my freedom and rehabilitation Matt is using drugs and keeps telling me about his life of crime. We then get a third cellie, Chucky. He is in for theft and a related probation violation. He is also a drug dealer, and even worse, a murderer, even though he was never caught or tried for it.

49

He relates to me how he murdered his girlfriend. Apparently, one night he gave his girlfriend a strong pain patch that he applied himself. She falls asleep from the drugs and wakes up begging him for help. (She is overdosing.) He does nothing. He literally watches her die. He says he was bored of her and it was just easier this way. I was stunned by this revelation and wondered how many reported "overdoses" are actually intentional murders.

Chucky and I talk a lot during my time in Kenai. He gets accepted into the RSAT[17] program which addresses drug and alcohol addiction. This program is key to measuring the success of Alaska's Department of Corrections (DOC). And funding of the DOC is impacted by these types of performance results. But the success of the program is more focused on enrollment in the program, and not on whether someone actually gets sober. I know of many guys who didn't actually have an addiction problem that were encouraged to took the class anyway. And since completing RSAT has a big impact on an inmate getting parole it's a very popular class and not hard to get guys to take it.

As you might imagine, confidentiality is an important part of RSAT. Under the presumption of confidentiality, Chucky has actually been honest in telling all of us in the class that he's been drinking and using drugs in prison and that he plans on continuing once he's released. Well, the counselors run and report Chucky's

---

[17] Residential Substance Abuse Treatment

confession to his Institutional Probation Officer. This is actually against the rules and doing so breaks confidentiality on every level.

Nonetheless, it was too late and Chucky was denied parole because of his honesty. As you might have guessed, most the guys saw what telling the truth got Chucky, so rather than being honest about their addiction they hide it so they can just make parole and get out.

QUESTION:

Do you think not fully overcoming addiction is one reason recidivism is such a serious problem?

Can you really blame an inmate for lying if the choice is honesty vs. getting out of prison?

In the meantime, I'm hired as a law librarian and as a caretaker of a Native inmate who didn't have the use of his legs. I'm doing very well. Everyday I'm reading the statutes and case law and as I do this, I'm learning there is corruption in the prison system. I am reading about prison policies and procedures and I realize that there are lots of rules and even laws being broken. After seeing it firsthand, I start coming for answers and the staff have no idea, so I start writing the COs for their take on things wondering what I am missing. And I am helping other inmates fight their write-ups and working on their classes for them so they can get out of here and be with their families.

I'm asking basic, innocent questions at first so no one will suspect what I am up to. However, even with my agenda to uncover potential corruption and poor management, I'm actually following the judge's orders and the Pre-Sentence Reports (PSR[18]) to a T.

Judges make up a large part of the backbone of the whole correctional system. I have a ton of questions:

- Why are judges so important to the system?
- Should probation officers follow everything judges say to do, like nearly all do?
- Why are PSRs done?
- Are the PSRs closely taken into account after they're submitted to the judge?
- If the inmate is expected to follow the judge's orders and the PSR, then does the system, run by the COs and the POs[19], assist the inmate in following these critical pieces of the rehabilitation process?
- If not, then how is the system going to actually rehabilitate people sent to prison? What is the point otherwise?

---

[18] A PSR is a report prepared by a probation officer to help the judge decide what sentence to give. It is used to find out about an offender's background.
[19] Parole Officer.

At my sentencing I'm told on the record by my judge that if I listen to him and do exactly what he says that, "Shane, you will be a productive member of society, but you have to follow what I'm telling you to do." I did follow his advice. However, I didn't just want to be a "productive" member of society, I wanted to be a "model" member of society.

I credit my late step-dad, Virgel Meinzer, AKA "Bosco," who was a police officer, for instilling in me the wisdom of doing what the judge says. He told me that, "If a judge says something to you, then you listen and you do it." This good man took me to court with him when I was a boy and taught me that if you don't respect the judge he can throw you in jail if he wants to. He also has the power to let you go.

So, I applied that wisdom and took things further on my own. For example, instead of just taking one state-certified anger management classes as ordered by the judge, I took at least another five programs that had anger management training included in the classes, one of which was a great class called Inside-Out Dad.

INNER WORKINGS OF A BROKEN SYSTEM

However, at the time I was not only taking the most important classes the Alaska DOC had to offer, but I was also learning the whole broken system from start to finish. And I started to realize that since I would be coming up for parole in a few years I shouldn't show up unprepared or empty-handed.

No. I'm coming with a full arsenal of evidence comparing my actions and behavior against everything the judge ordered me to do. I would have every piece of paper or cop-out I had written and received over my time in lock-up. My preparation would be so thorough that the COs would have to either lie to keep me in there or provide contrary evidence showing that I didn't follow the orders and guidance from the PSR or the judge's orders. I needed to prove my ultimate argument, which was: "Since I'm doing so well in here why not let me out?"

I learn later that inmates represent a large stream of income to the State. According to a 2015 report[20], only six states spent more taxpayer dollars on inmates than Alaska, more than $315,000,000, which works out to be $429 per Alaskan resident, by far the highest in the country. So, from the State's perspective it's hard to look at the prison population and not see dollar signs. The more prisoners there are the more money is allocated to operating prisons.

---

[20] www.vera.org The Price of Prisons Report, 2015.

And the bigger the budget the harder it is to spot missing or misallocated monies.

Sure, the stated purpose of incarceration in "correctional" centers is to protect the public from dangerous people and, secondarily, to "correct" or rehabilitate men and women who have committed serious crimes to become better people and not commit crime again. However, I think whenever you insert a financial motive into keeping someone locked up the decision to release them becomes harder. I hate to think of how many people are still locked up because parole boards and prison administrators get fuzzy about what is really in the best interest of society. (I think with privately-run prisons it's even more of a problem. More on that someday.)

But back to my situation. I know that through my actions, my behavior, and my efforts to become something more than just a "productive" member of society I was giving myself every shot at being paroled and showing that I had succeeded. In fact, not only was I not adding to the failure of the system, actually, I was showing the way that incarceration could and should really work. By simply following the judge's orders and PSR, just like every inmate is supposed to do, I was able to rehabilitate, correct course, and exit prison ready to be productive in society and contribute to my local economy and community.

Imagine if tens of thousands of guys like me were able to do this! Surely the financial benefit of **criminals** exiting prison and becoming ***contributors*** to the economy would outweigh any financial incentive to keep us locked up.

So, with this new realization and deep determination pushing me forward, I carry on doing my best. I still have never received a write-up, even though I have been set-up a couple times. I ended up beating those false accusations because of my ability to follow the basic principles of the whole system, like video cameras. For, example, if someone said I did something, and I knew I hadn't, I would "push paper" asking the COs to check the video footage from their multi-million-dollar camera system which is designed to protect the inmates and correctional staff. I used the same important tool the prison was using to prove any accusers wrong and stay out of any unnecessary trouble.

I'm ready to fight for what is right in here, but it's getting kind of dangerous for me. I realize they may be catching on that I've been gathering information and using the mail to send some of the information about their failings to attorneys and state and local officials I thought should care and could do something about it. I realize money is missing. I just do not know how much or where it is coming from or going to. I do know things are not being done right.

I also know the Federal Government is funding most, if not all, of these rehabilitative programs. I learn that running these programs is a very lucrative enterprise. I find out that the programming I have taken costs about $250,000! And I now realize that taxpayers and inmate's families pay for these programs to help their loved ones, the inmate, and is one of the most important factors in reducing recidivism and enacting prison reform.

I'm gobbling up all of this information. I also realize I'm a walking pain-in-the-butt, simply because I'm just following the rules but also carefully asking questions. And I am still confused about a few things:

- How much money is disappearing or being wasted?
- How can these prisons just spend taxpayers' money so freely without results?
- Is recidivism declining?
- How are they teaching all these classes, without a change in recidivism numbers at all?
- How can they always blame the inmates for the lack of positive change?
- Don't the people running all the costly programs have any accountability?

My head is spinning thinking about how much money is being spent for so little improvement. While I don't understand everything that is going on, I am confident that I am uniquely positioned to uncover and expose important information that could help change the way things are being done. I have written proof and I'm one of the very few write-up free inmates in here which gives me credibility and "freedom" to move around inside.

I have started to look into how they run their system and it's clearly flawed from beginning to end. I know it's not right and I'm coming full-force to try to help the staff make better decisions. Obviously, I am not responsible for the decisions of staff members and they have to sleep in whatever beds they make, so to speak, but I am hopeful that by letting them know that prison rules are being broken they may take more ownership in making sure they are followed more regularly.

When I see that rules are being broken, I send cop-outs to the staff asking about these issues. The response would tell me if they even knew or cared they were breaking the rules. I'm bugged and wanting to know why the correctional staff aren't being held to the same standards of compliance as we inmates are. I am not the only inmate working hard to follow the judge's orders but I am keenly aware that doing so is the best way to my getting out of here ASAP and seeing my family again. I am working a lot, doing my programming, writing letters to my family, and getting no write-ups. All of which is expected of every inmate and reflects the best use of taxpayer funds, allocated in the hundreds of millions per year, to helping inmates rehabilitate and get back into society.

QUESTION:

Should taxpayer dollars continue to be used for programs that are not effective in reducing recidivism?

THE COMPANY YOU KEEP

One of the worst things about being in prison is the company you keep. And the company gets worse as you move from a medium-security facility to a maximum-security prison. And as I have mentioned, Alaska doesn't have the death penalty, so no death row, which means that truly the worst of the worst, rather than being executed, serve out their life sentences with guys like me. Over my time in prison I am sent to Seward, Alaska's maximum-security prison, four different times. It's still hard to wrap my head around how a guy like me, no doubt convicted of a serious crime, could be placed in the same facility as someone truly evil. Someone like Robert Christian Hansen, aka the "Butcher Baker[21]."

"Bob the Butcher," as we knew him in Seward, was infamous. He was an American serial killer. For twelve years (1971-1983) he abducted, raped, and murdered at least 17 women in and around Anchorage. He hunted his victims, largely sex workers in Alaska for the oil boom, like wild animals with a hunting rifle and knife, and eventually a bow and arrow.

The Butcher Baker was married with two small kids and owned a bakery downtown, frequented by local law enforcement. His M.O. was to solicit sex workers, because they weren't as likely to be missed, then abduct them and chain them from the ceiling in his home where he would

---

[21] https://www.aetv.com/real-crime/alaska-serial-killer-robert-hansen

rape and torture them repeatedly. Then he would fly the girl in his bush plane to a remote location where he would set the girl loose and then hunt her until he killed her. His savage, terrifying crimes were the subject of a 2013 film called "The Frozen Ground." Actor John Cusack played the part of Bob the Butcher and Nicholas Cage played an Alaskan State trooper looking into the killings.

He was sentenced to life *plus* 461 years. When I was there, he could often be seen freely strutting around the prison with his cane. I met him several times.

He died in 2014 at the age of 75.

Another Serial Killer?

I also had the interesting but unfortunate opportunity to meet a notorious murderer named Joshua Wade. We met in Anchorage when I was being transported. He was famously hot-tempered and killed two women in Anchorage. One in 2007 and the other in 2000. He confessed to the earlier murder when he was convicted of the murder he committed in 2007.

As I have noted already, Alaska doesn't have the death penalty but due to the fact that the 2007 murder also involved bank fraud, a federal crime, the federal government could pursue the death penalty against Wade if authorities could prove the bank fraud was related to the murder of this victim, Mindy Schloss. He would have been the first prisoner in the history of the Alaska prison system to face the death penalty.

Ultimately, he was sentenced to life without a possibility for parole. In the summer of 2014, when we were in Seward together, he claimed he was being mistreated in the hole there and struck a deal for a transfer to a federal prison in Indiana. In exchange for the transfer, he admitted to the murders of three men in Anchorage and claimed he committed his first murder when he was only 14 years old. Scary, and really sad.

It is still unclear if he was actually a serial killer, or not. But if he was, he was driven by his intense anger and not some sick, cunning M.O. And no one actually knows if he killed more victims than he confessed to killing. And the families of his victims don't care if he was a serial killer or not because that won't bring their loved one back but it's a fascinating mystery.

Joshua was a handsome guy; clean-cut, soft voice. We met and talked several times. I was on the phone next to him one day and overhead him say that all he cared about was his music because it brought life to the living conditions in prison. Since being locked-up in a federal maximum-security prison in the Midwest he has been classified as "one of the most assaultive, predatory, riotous, or seriously disruptive prisoners."

There is an excellent article by Robin Barefield on Medium[22] with many more details about Joshua Wade if you ever want to learn more.

---

[22] https://medium.com/@robinbarefield76/alaska-serial-killer-joshua-wade-dcf79b9aa6b4

MY BROTHER'S BROTHER

While I lived in the same facilities with some really scary dudes, I mostly met and got to know lots of young men who came from really troubled backgrounds. And when you take the time to understand their circumstances you start to feel some compassion for them. Nothing excuses or justifies crime, especially violent crimes, but life is rarely as simple as black and white, good and bad.

I am including here an account written in 2011 by one of these young men that I knew well on the inside. His name is Kevin and he has given me permission to share his story, in his own unedited words. He is a fellow brother in Christ who tragically lost his own brother to the wicked ways of the world. I met him at Wildwood in Kenai and we became good friends. He taught me how to play handball and was very persistent in talking to the Chaplain here to get me in the Alpha program which changed my life. God bless you, Kevin.

THE DAY MY BROTHER WAS KILLED

The day was July 16th 2010; nothing out of the ordinary going on, my cellmate, Shane, was a really good friend of mine. I was incarcerated at Wildwood Pre-trial facility. I was in this pod where you're locked down for 2 hrs at a time it's called tier racking, where one tier is let out at a time to use the phones, watch TV, shower, etc.

The reason I was locked up this time was 60 days prior to this I was released and put in a treatment facility named Serenity House, due to my severe drug addiction. I ended up getting kicked out, and they wanted me to wait there until the next day so they could talk to my lawyer to see what was going to happen to me. I was probably going back to jail. So I didn't stick around. There are too many events leading up to my arrest to get into any detail, but I'll give it to you in a nutshell.

I have a brother he's 2 years older than me, I was 19 I think when all this happened, anyways, he was staying at a friend of ours house over on K-Beach road, his names Dean. Somehow my girlfriend Alexis and I ended up over there, at this time I have warrants out for my arrest and so does she.

Well we got pulled over at the end of Deans driveway, because on our way here we had been in a church parking lot making a drug deal, when a State Trooper had pulled in, well the person I was meeting went one way (towards Kenai) And we went the other (towards Soldotna) well Deans driveway was only a mile or two up the road, well they had called in for backup and said we were "Running From Them" Which wasn't the case at all, we were just too high to comprehend the what was going on.

So they surrounded us and they asked for all of our names, well I panicked because I had warrants and so did my girlfriend so when he got to me I rattled off the only name I could think of, and know the birth date of the name. My brother Brendan. He was sitting 250 feet up the driveway in Dean's cabin. My girlfriend also had warrants and she gave a false name as well.

Well little did I know the person I had met in the parking lot to sell drugs too would give them my real name. So shortly after they let us go she calls me and tells me to get out of there that the cops were coming back, well me being high on drugs, this kind of spooked me a little bit. Well Dean tells me to chill out, and come inside and chill with Alexis. Well shortly after I look up at the camera (He has a camera on his driveway) and sure enough here comes the whole Department of State Troopers with their guns drawn.

Long story short, this was the last time I got to see my brother, in Handcuffs. On my way to prison for using a false name and for my warrants. The last words my brother said to me were "I Love You Kev" and I being angry at him said some pretty bad stuff back, which I regret now. I was so lost in my own world that I didn't pay any attention to the "real world" the word "Normal" to me means drugs and guns. There's a lot more to the story kind of "behind the scenes" stuff that I may get into a little more detail later.

So here I sit at Wildwood, booked on charges of violating conditions of release and giving false information to a peace officer. So here I am in this crappy pod where we've got to lockdown majority of the day, they let us out every 2 hours, and for food. I overhear these guys talking about a shooting over on K-Beach road, at that time I didn't even think about it, I just thought it was another one of those things that didn't involve me. Little did I know, I was gravely mistaken.

It was about noon, on July 16th 2010. I remember every detail about the day, like it was yesterday. The Correctional officer came to the door and said McGee, get dressed and come with me, so I followed her out of my cell, out of the mod, and down big staircase leading to the booking office. She put me in this little room with a phone in it, and she said "when it rings pick it up". When I picked up the phone, I recognized my mother's voice, she was hysterical.

I remember she was saying "They Shot Him" and I kept asking her who. She said your brother, the cops shot him. At this time she didn't know who shot him, all she knew is her eldest son was shot dead. So here I am in this tiny room, no bigger than 5x5 with a table and a phone on it. And it's really hot..., I did the only thing I knew to do. I reacted with rage, and anger. My only brother I've got is dead, and for all I know it was the cops who put me in here who did it, so at that time I was really angry with everyone.

Well I later found out that it wasn't the Police who shot and killed my older brother, but it was a Local lunatic

*who had a past history of firearms and drugs. To top this
all off, my brother wasn't alone when he got killed. His best
friend Tom was there with him. I guess he got shot over 500
bucks; well it was actually over a 500 dollar assault rifle
called an SKS. I guess the guy walked into the cabin after
knocking on the door, my brother's friend answered the
door, and he walked in.*

*He asked my brother where his cell phone was and
why he wasn't answering it, my brother told him it had
gotten stolen the night before, and the guy said Bullshit. He
then asked Brendan about the SKS, and he told him the
same thing, I guess my brother went to get up off the couch
and that's when he shot him in the face with a 12 gauge
shotgun. Thomas turned around and waited to be shot too,
but the guy just left. So Thomas immediately locked the
door and called 911 and sat down next to my brother until
the paramedics had gotten there, he was presumed dead
instantly after the gunshot.*

*The guy's name is Lyle Ludvick. I actually had to
look at him every day, through the glass of course when I
was in pretrial, he was in another mod. There was a
Manhunt for him following the shooting it lasted about two
weeks until they found, and arrested him. He even had a
standoff with the police at a local trailer park in Sterling.
But after negotiating, he gave himself up.*

*He's currently awaiting trial, and is incarcerated at
Wildwood Pre-Trial Facility, on charges of Second Degree*

Murder. I still don't understand to this day, why he's only charged with second degree murder, it sure seems like it should be first. I mean come on, he went to where my brother was at with a loaded 12 gauge shotgun, and he knew exactly what he was going to do. Sure my brother wasn't perfect, none of us are. He did his fair share of drug using, and ripping people off, but that comes with the dope game.

He wasn't given a fair trial, this Lyle guy was the Judge, and the jury, and unfortunately the executioner..... I hope whoever reads this understands the seriousness of drugs, and guns. In one day, my whole life changed just because of this one fellow who wasn't obviously thinking about the immediate consequences of his actions. I hope you guys like my story. Thank you.

Kevin M. 2011

I want everyone, but the kids especially, to know, that I asked Kevin to write this for you. It was very difficult for him, because the last words he said to his brother were hurtful. Of course, he didn't know they would be his last words but he deeply regrets what he said to his brother. What he wanted to say, and should have said was, "I love you, Dean." Unfortunately, there is nothing he can do about that lost moment, ever.

However, there is something *you* can do:

69

- Stop doing drugs.
- Tell the ones closest to you, "I love you."
- Start being a part of their lives.

Take it from me, you do not want to be where I was, locked up. And you do not want to be where Kevin's brother is.

Everything I am sharing in my writings is real and there are so many examples of what not to do. So please, "STOP!!" before this happens to you.

I promise, if you continue doing drugs, it is just a matter of time before a tragedy like Kevin's touches your life somehow.

ALPHA MALES

I meet Kris a couple weeks into my time at
Wildwood in Kenai. At this point, I had about five years
left in my prison sentence. I am just trying to make it as
best I can day-to-day. I see an aura on this kid, Kris. He's
young, solid smile, and working hard in this class, Alpha.

We hit it off and he asks me if I would like to join
Alpha. I ask him a few questions and he tells me that
usually to get into this class you have to have less than two
years left before your release. He answers, "You still have a
long time left but I'll ask the chaplain for you."

Kris comes back and tells me they are going to
allow me to join Alpha based on my good behavior and
reputation in the prison. Because they are making an
exception on my release date, they give me a few
conditions that I have to adhere to, such as: make a six-
month commitment to the program; stay employed; stay out
of trouble; and actively participate in the group discussions.
I agree to every condition and kept them all.

Now I'm just waiting for the move. Kenai is
overflowing with inmates; people are literally sleeping on
the floors. So, it was an unusual situation but the only place
for some of us to stay was in a room, not a locked cell like
usual, downstairs on the first floor. This floor is where all
the programming happens so I get a close-up look at all the
programs. I get to see the way the system is run and all of

its pros and cons. I am excited for the change and what seems like a good opportunity.

Well, Kris and I start talking and hanging out a lot. He is only 21 at the time but I can see potential in this kid. He shares with me the major issues his family is dealing with. (Sadly, those issues will get worse.) But Kris is spunky, smiles a lot, and is staying sober. He is a local and knows everyone. There are all kinds of drugs and alcohol around but he stays sober. We walk the track, talk, and study. I'm pushing him to succeed and he is pushing me.

We have mentor night once a week in Alpha. This is where men from the outside come inside to visit and try to help the inmates feel a little hope and make a plan for when they are released. The mentors help us prepare for life on the outside and get setup for success; they will help us find work, a place to live, a church to attend, and just a good solid place to hang out and hopefully stay out of trouble. They talk about the Lord and our lives within these walls. Kris has me meet his mentor my first night of mentor night. We visit for a bit and I find out that Kris' mentor is a big leader in the program and is helping as best as he can.

I am impressed and realize people do care and am grateful they are here spending their time trying to help us. The next week I get my mentor, John. He and I talk and visit in the prison. After a few weeks he passes me his number so we can start talking on the phone as well. He is a builder by trade. With a mentor like this in my corner I feel pretty confident that I will be able to handle anything bad that may happen from now until I get out.

The guys in Alpha are held to a higher standard than the rest of the prisoners. We are expected to take care of ourselves better than everyone else, watch our language, and behave as examples for all to see.

The time moves so slowly here and it feels like it will be forever before I am released but I just try to focus on getting home and I recognize the importance of all the classes, policies and procedures. John knows I am working hard to get home because I have all my support there. To me "getting home" at that point means being transferred out of Alaska to a prison closer to home.

Remember that all of my family is in Washington, not here in Alaska. Frankly, one of the driving reasons for my good behavior is that I am hoping, the entire time I am locked up, that I will be able to get transferred to my home state so that I can see my family and they can visit me much more regularly. I think, "If I just stay write-up free, follow the orders, and complete the programming they will have to send me to Washington to finish my sentence." I was wrong to think this.

QUESTION:

Is it wrong for a prisoner to be able to serve their time near family if he works hard to contribute to the order of the prison and maximize his rehabilitation for the benefit of society upon re-entry?

Prisons advocate family involvement in the rehabilitation process. Why keep them apart then? Shouldn't this be a consideration *while* incarcerated?

In fact, the system and the programming I am taking all emphasize the importance of family relationships in rehabilitating during incarceration and post-release. But despite my exemplary behavior they never work out a transfer to Washington. This would have relieved such a burden on my loved ones, and me. I still do not understand why this happened but it took an emotional toll on me, and most unfortunately, my children. All I really wanted to do was learn about Jesus so that I could make my life better and get home to be closer to my kids.

There was a time while I was in Kenai when my family came to visit for a few days and it meant the absolute world to me: my mom Carrie, brother Nathan, sister Rachel, and my daughter Ashley. It was summertime and I remember having so much fun and laughter.

TROUBLE IN ALPHA

Alpha class is actually pretty hard. We meet five days a week and have books to read, and homework and personal assignments to do. I'm in Alpha for a few months when I first meet a man I'll call Abaddon. I met him when he was still upstairs, not downstairs with us. He talked a lot and right away I could tell he was a sociopath and a compulsive liar. He would just say outrageous lies and it was amazing how firmly he pretended to believe what he was saying. I knew he knew I could see right through him and his lies.

A couple of weeks later I hear he is coming to Alpha class and I knew problems would come with him. Sometimes people have to learn the hard way. Almost immediately Abaddon is in the class up talking like he was a preacher. (Don't get me wrong, preaching is a great thing as long as you're the student and not an inmate acting like the warden.) I could tell people liked him but I also knew his mindset wasn't right. I noticed he would approach, or sort of recruit, the weaker inmates; the ones that were left out, so he could have some backing if or when he needed it. I started hearing some of these guys say how wonderful he was and how he wanted to make things in Alpha better.

It was clear to me that he was coming after the prison Chaplain who ran the Alpha program, looking to replace him. But I knew his plot wouldn't be easy to carry out. The Alpha class is mainly facilitator-led discussions of faith with each member taking a turn to share. And the way

75

Abaddon hijacked conversations and talked over guys when they were talking raised questions. A leader helps another person talk through things, not trample on your couple minutes.

The next thing I noticed that revealed his scheme to me was that he went after the leaders of Alpha, challenged them. I could tell that he was sowing the seeds of division and that things were going to get bad. And, that's *exactly* what happened. I think he knew that I knew what he was up to so in class he would look down to avoid making eye contact with me. And the truth is that there was nothing bad he could say about me. I was doing what we all were supposed to do. A couple of the other inmates told me he was talking crap about me to them. But the guys in Alpha told him straight away that they liked me. That was costly for him. These guys were loyal to me because I always tried to help them when I could.

As a result of this loyalty the guys started to feel an animosity towards Abaddon. That's when it started to get really interesting. He was pushing for changes but I pointed out that, even though things weren't perfect, how things run was the decision of the Chaplain. It's his program and that should be that. Since most of the group was starting to see what Abaddon was really up to—a thinly veiled takeover of Alpha—he started to realize that he wasn't going to get what he wanted as easily as he had planned, if at all.

That said, there were a few of the guys that thought the program was not being run effectively. So, the Chaplain had to deal with some issues for a time and it was tense. Word about the tension in the Alpha program started to make its way through the prison. The Chaplain definitely ran things his way and Abaddon, with the support of the guys who agreed with him, kept trying to tell the Chaplain how he should run things. Finally, in a come-to-Jesus meeting, which I simply listened to, the group tossed Abaddon and we went about our day.

A few years later at Goose Creek in Wassila I see Abaddon on the yard still working to tear things down instead of build them up. Some people just never change.

LAST HAIRCUT...EVER?

It's late 2014 and I am in the hole at Goose Creek again. Other than getting out of the hole, the only thing I have to look forward to in this mind-numbing state is my daily shower. To keep my sanity, I sing songs from my childhood during my few moments alone in there:

"This little light of mine, I'm going to let it shine."
"Jesus loves me this I know."
"The itsy-bitsy spider climbed up the water spout."
"Amazing grace, how sweet the sound."

I can still almost hear my rendition of these sweet songs bouncing off the cold, lonely walls of the prison. Luckily, no one yelled at me so they must have just tolerated it.

You should know that at this point in my incarceration I'm a short timer and have served most of my sentence. I've followed the various laws, codes and rules. I have no write-ups. As such, I am eligible for furlough, basically ankle monitoring, so I am really trying to keep my nose clean and avoid anything that would set me back. I still had no write-ups, super rare in Alaska, and to keep it that way, I actually took myself out of general and *requested* to be locked in the hole for a couple months. And now I'm nearly to the door.

78

As you might imagine in prison, haircuts and personal care services aren't exactly the highest priority or some relaxing experience of personal pampering. But we can get free haircuts and since I am getting out soon, I decide to get my last haircut on the inside. I can't even remember how long it had been since my last haircut. So, here goes.

My adrenaline is running high. I know the system has done me and lots of others wrong so I am on high alert to be sure nothing messes up my release. My first haircut, a harrowing experience I wrote about in my first book, is a distant memory since it was so long ago. I write a cop-out requesting a haircut. It's granted and, before I know it, it's my turn for a haircut. A couple of guards come to my cell, one of them tells me to turn around, and slaps the handcuffs on me. Since I am only a few months from getting out of here and seeing my kids and family, I follow directions even more closely than usual. I can't give the guards any reason, however small, to write me up or cause me any trouble that could delay my release.

They handcuff me through the tray slot, open the door, and lead me by the arm to the main segregation room. As I walk by, all the other inmates there in the hole are watching. There is literally nothing else to do except look through our little window when something is going on outside the cell. They take me through the maze of doors and halls down to the prison barber. We finally get to the door of the room and it's locked. The COs find the right key on their huge keyring and open the door. We walk through the door and I see the barber.

"Holy crap! It can't be!" There stands the barber at over 6 feet tall, weighing at least 300 lbs. Guess who? It's the Hammer!!!! I'm screaming inside, "Nooooo flippin' way!" I only have 2 months left and this guy scares me. Huge guy in here for life with a sharp blade around my head and neck? My hands are handcuffed behind my back as the COs sit me in the chair. Then they lock the door behind them as they leave. Gulp…

As I sat there with the Hammer using his sharp scissors inches from my jugular, I was totally OK that he didn't mention our first haircut over six years earlier when he exploded in rage. But I am pretty sure he remembered. And trust me, I know I did. I thank God nothing happened that day and that I lived through what I thought could have been my last haircut…ever.

MATT

I'm in Kenai still with my cellie Matt. Remember him? The genius that brought a stolen arsenal of weapons to a motel. Well he's still telling me all about his volatile life of crime. I'm trying to get into the Alpha program to work on my faith in God and he's relating stories of robbing churches, selling drugs through US customs, and becoming a big-time drug dealer on the Alaska Peninsula.

Apparently, he meets a Jamaican drug dealer and starts getting kilos of cocaine hidden in computers shipped to him here in Alaska. The Jamaican comes to Alaska to hang out with Matt. One night they are at a bar and the Jamaican runs into a guy who owes him money. There's an argument and the Jamaican pulls a gun, shoots him in the leg, and he and Matt rob him in an effort to get back the Jamaican's money. They hurry away from the scene of the crime and the Jamaican gets on a plane and leaves.

Some time passes and Matt heads to Jamaica to meet his dealer and partner. They have quite the business going as they send drugs through the mail and, before they know it, they are living the high life. But, there's always a dark side to the high life fueled by illegal businesses. Another argument over money happens in Jamaica with some guy and this time the Jamaican shoots the guy in the head. In broad daylight.

This shook Matt. As a front-row seat to a brazen, cold-blooded murder like this would shake anyone. But,

81

unfortunately, not enough. Matt still continues to supply the Peninsula and the State of Alaska with cocaine. Matt is known throughout Alaska for supplying high quality product and this reputation actually leads to one night that will haunt him for the rest of his life.

He is home and a so-called friend named Ruth shows up wanting 10 ounces of coke. They set a place to meet and when Matt shows up several people jump him. They beat him severely: they break ribs, give him a concussion, and leave him for dead. Matt survives but ends up in the hospital for a while recovering from this beating. The people who jumped him are never caught.

He gets out of the hospital and Matt can't help himself and goes right back to selling drugs. However, Ruth shows up again at his house, presumably to set him up again, and things take a fateful, irreversible turn. They argue and Matt shoves a shotgun in her mouth, knocking out her front teeth. He thinks about pulling the trigger to just be done with her. But she is screaming and crying and there's blood streaming from her mouth.

"Please don't kill me!"

He pulls the gun out of her mouth, yells at her to get lost and to never come back.

Ruth is gone but Matt's trouble that night is just starting. One of the guys that robbed him before had come to Matt's house with her but stayed behind in the car. This is the biggest and final mistake this guy ever makes.

Even though Ruth is now dealt with, Matt keeps his guard up and is ready for this guy. The guy enters the house and Matt kills him. He then proceeds to burn down the house to destroy all the evidence. He takes the body of the dude he just killed and puts it in a barrel with diesel fuel and quicklime. Then he puts the body in the guy's own car and drives into the deep woods to bury it. He ditches the car into a sinkhole, never to be found.

Meanwhile, unaware of what happened that night after she fled Matt's house, Ruth continued to lead a drug-fueled, risky lifestyle probably trying to find some sort of peace, or even happiness, in her life. Tragically she never found it and about a year later, in July 2015, she parked her car outside of the Spring Creek Prison in Seward and demanded that all the murderers be released and, when that didn't happen, she blew her head off.

The inmates had heard about a girl who had shot herself outside the prison walls and I asked Matt about it. He told me it was Ruth. He went on to say he was glad she did it and, "good riddance."

THE VETERAN

I'm working in the law library in Kenai and I meet the "Veteran." He's an ornery old guy who talks incessantly about sovereignty and living off the grid. But he's interesting and we talk a lot. At this time, I have started to write my prison experiences that will eventually fill the pages of this book and others. Everyone knows that I am going to write a book and I'm spending whatever free time I have on it.

Also, I'm writing judges and politicians and sending 15 to 20 letters out a week at first. That increased to 30 to 40 letters a week as I was getting feedback that my letters were helping some people so I wrote more. Stamps cost $0.50 and I'm only making $0.50 per hour so I am working one hour to send out one letter. (All the rest of my money was going to my family.)

The Veteran is writing lots of letters, too. He teaches me that stamps are like money. Since they are issued by the federal government you can exchange them for cash. So, the more stamps I have the more money I have. This is a new hustle for me. We actually start gambling for stamps while I'm working in the law library. The irony!

And, by the way, out of that $0.50 per hour I make working, $0.25 is being deducted for child support. I would find out later that hundreds and hundreds of dollars never made it to my children. After my release, I brought the missing funds up to my probation officer since I had the paperwork to prove it. He said, "We will get it back to you." It's been five years and I'm still waiting. LOL.

It's amazingly frustrating that if I, as a parolee, miss an appointment, even unintentionally, they can send me to jail. If hundreds of dollars of child support payments go "missing" and I am told "we'll get it back to you," but they never do then I have to ask: where is the justice? Where is the accountability? I know life isn't fair but, come on, guys!

Also, of the $0.50 per hour I am earning at my jobs, $0.05 is going into my savings, just like a regular savings account you can withdraw when you are released. I had a $5.00 per month cable bill. Yes, I got to watch TV in prison as a privilege for my good behavior and hard work. My family bought the TV for me as a birthday present when I was in Seward. But I'm about the only guy I know of who actually paid the cable bill. Everyone scammed the system and didn't pay. Well, I did pay and the guys gave me crap for it.

So, after all those expenses were taken out of my pay there wasn't much leftover for stamps so I could keep sending my letters. I needed a way to earn stamps So, we start gambling for stamps. At first, the stakes are four or five stamps but after a while we were gambling for twenty stamps. That's how I got stamps for my 30 to 40 letters.

Meanwhile, I'm working on math skills with the same guy that I called the "Punk" in my first book. We are doing flash cards that I made when I was a GED instructor. The Punk was learning how to do multiplication and he was getting the tables down pretty well. Remember, he had schizophrenia and he was almost killed not long ago so he was skittish and laying low.

So, there are two shifts in the law library at Kenai and I have the day shift. Another guy has the evening shift since I had all my Alpha classes in the evening. I'm working my shift one day and a couple of guys come up telling me that the staff had just destroyed my room. This kind of search happens from time-to-time but, on this occasion, they literally destroyed my room from top to bottom.

What I didn't know is that someone had stolen a recording device from the library. This device was used for inmates to send and receive messages from their attorneys or to listen to court hearings. The device is locked up and there are only two keys; I have one and the night shift guy has the other one. Well, he stole it but gave some story about how I had done it. So, I'm targeted by the staff as the culprit. And that's why they ransacked my room. I am, of course, bugged and upset. To find the truth all they had to do was check the video footage and they could see that the device was never used during my shift the past few days so it couldn't have been me.

Well, they decide to lock down the whole prison and initiate "tier racking[23]." The guards are going room to room taking everything they find. Inmates are pissed off at me because, a) the prison is shut down because they think I stole a recorder, and b) they think I said something about the guys who are getting their rooms trashed. I am like a deer in the headlights. I had nothing to do with this and know nothing about what is going on.

The guards are busting guys with "pruno[24]" or prison wine, weed, tattooing, etc. all because of a missing device that I had nothing to do with. And the heat is on me from all sides. Thankfully, my so-called partner at the law library made a crucial mistake. On the video footage they can actually see him getting into the drawer where the device was kept, but they can't see him take it. However, he wrote a strange note explaining how the device was taken, which guys had it, and to whom it was sold but signing my name to make it look like I orchestrated the entire petty crime. This note would actually end up sealing his fate.

The staff do a deeper review of footage from all the cameras that would have had a view of his every move from the point they saw him getting into the drawer. Which rooms he went to. Which people he interacted with. The cameras actually catch him slipping the note under the door of one of the supervisors. I am told by a staff member that he had left the note. I was fortunate that the video revealed

---

[23] The guards only let one tier out at a time to use the phones, watch TV, shower, etc.
[24] Prison alcohol described as a "bile flavored wine cooler." https://en.wikipedia.org/wiki/Pruno

the truth. He actually let me read the note. I couldn't tell anyone the truth yet, even though everyone thought it was me and I was anxious to get the target off my back. The good news for me is this guy left a trail of clues that eventually exposed the truth that he had done it.

However, I was fired from my job at the law library while they finished their investigation. Once the prison is off lockdown and things are officially settled, I get my job back. Shortly thereafter, a guy who did tattoos in the prison pops his head in the door of the library and told me that when all this was going down, he and another dude were going to jump me. Thankfully the matter was resolved before they did.

And the cool thing is a couple of days later this same guy came back and I ended up helping him beat a write-up he had received. He was grateful and gave me a hug and, even better, a bunch of food worth like $10-that's 20 hours of work for me! I earned back respect from the guys and staff after that. The staff could see that I was actually trying so would be friendly and even say hello to me once in a while.

However, I am sure the guy that made this story up and caused all these problems, literally for the entire prison, still has many issues even to this day. But I am a forgiving guy who tries to show empathy and kindness to others, even those who have wronged me. So, while I was in Kairos, another faith-based program, I was given the chance to test my character. They gave us each a bag of really good food from the outside, which was a rarity. Most of the guys just ate the food themselves, and I really couldn't blame them.

However, the bags were supposed to be for us to give to someone who had done us wrong; someone who had betrayed us. I knew who I had to give my bag to. Without hesitation I went to the room of the guy who had tried to pin the law library theft on me. I said, "I'm not mad at you and want you to have this. I forgive you."

I walked out and never said another word about it to him or anyone else. I was asked if I had given away my food but I said nothing. The words on this page represent the first time I am sharing what I did.

CAMERON

I meet a guy named Cameron years earlier in Cook Inlet, which is a pre-trial facility in Anchorage, and he was the #2 most wanted criminal in Alaska and, not surprisingly, he did not play nice. I'm not sure if he was the best forger in the state or not but he was high on the most wanted list for good reason. We got to know each other and he told me his stories. He was a ruthless criminal whose specialties included outright robbery, creating fake IDs, forging both business and personal checks, mailbox schemes, and carrying weapons.

While he is telling me his stories, I am helping him progress in school. He was smart. Together, we tackled his GED classes. He started to change and talk about God. You don't become Alaska's second most wanted without a long list of crimes, so he was no joke. But despite his deeds he told me that he believed in God.

We keep studying and talking about God. He comes to terms with his destructive criminal past and commits to leaving it behind. He graduates and finishes his GED! I'm super proud of him. Then, while still in prison for his crimes committed in Alaska, his federal crimes finally catch up with him and he gets arrested by the Feds about six months later.

I got a few letters a couple years later. He told me he missed me and explained everything about how the Feds charged him for the same things he had told me. He said he actually was relieved for getting in trouble and expressed remorse for his life of crime. He assured me he still loved God. I smiled huge when I read his letter.

PAUL

I meet a guy named Paul in Kenai and he was working for a railroad as a "bridgeman," responsible for the maintenance and operation of bridges on the railroad line. He had worked for the railroad for years and was a senior-level executive. His dad got him his first job at the company many years before.

Paul had a major drinking problem which led to multiple DWIs and he eventually received a felony conviction. In prison Paul had become a main leader in the Alpha program. He taught me lots about the Bible in this role. We talked dozens of times and had Bible studies together on numerous occasions.

Paul had heard that I was helping guys to get their GEDs. He told me he didn't have his. So, I told him to come on by and we would get him all fixed up. So, Paul and I worked on the issues he needed to address in order for him to advance. Once we knew what he needed to do, he advanced really fast and was ready for the GED test in no time. He took the test and was ranked in the top 90% in Alaska. Now that he was a high school graduate Paul started talking about taking college classes when I moved again. It was deeply rewarding to see Paul do so well and stay motivated to keep going.

I was in a good spot, happy and progressing, but it seems like life, through God, always has something coming our way to give us a chance to grow. The problem is that usually that "thing" usually looks like a struggle.

ADAM

Nearly every day from 7AM to 10PM I'm working three jobs, including as law librarian. I am also taking classes, and, in fact, I just passed a college pre-test so I could start taking college classes. I'm a very busy man and inmates are starting to talk with me all the time. Probably because I always tried to cheer people up and shine some light in an otherwise very dark place. I'm doing so well that I get asked to be the Chaplain's Helper by my peers and the Chaplain.

I decide to accept the job but had to step down as the law librarian since the hours conflicted. I keep growing. Lots of inmates start to come to me asking for advice or just to shoot the breeze. There are lots of different faces and almost as many bible studies. I was loving the Bible. I loved the guys. And they would come to me to include me in their studies. However, this period of happiness and progress is about to be cut short thanks to another inmate.

I'm living with Adam and he is also an Alpha member. He is high strung and hot-tempered. We do bible studies and visits. He tells me he's a little jealous of me because I was working hard, had lots going on, and he knew I was moving forward. I'm actually trying to help him make progress, too but his nature and demeanor are holding him back. Our relationship is tense.

One day in the chapel I'm working as usual. There are always guys coming up to visit and check in. However,

94

this one day, a dude named Timothy wrote an insult about Adam on the chalk board. I told Timothy to erase it. He did. But when I stepped out someone else wrote it on the board again and trouble is about to start.

I had gone to my room to take a 15-minute power nap. I'm worn out. The three jobs. Working hard in Alpha and the other programs I am in. The mentoring I'm doing to help guys get their parole packets. I'm working very hard to get out of here when it's time. And I'm pooped.

I'm just shutting my eyes and little do I know, Adam has come into the chapel and reads his name on the board with lots of insults about him. His temper lights up and he's almost fighting other inmates, and threatens a couple guys upstairs. People are trying, in vain, to get him to calm down.

Adam is really mad and he's coming for me because he wrongly assumes that I had something to do with those insulting things written about him. He is unaware that I was actually the one who told Timothy to erase those words off the board. So, I'm lying in my bed and the door flies open and he's coming for me. Suddenly all I can hear is Adam yelling and threats coming out of his mouth. He says something about the insults about him on the chalk board in the Chapel.

I'm in prison and some of the meanest, most violent guys on the planet are around me. I jump up not knowing what's going on or who's coming for me. Adam's nostrils are flaring, his breathing is heavy, and his eyes are wide open like a raging bull. I'm trying like a matador to avoid this bull but my room isn't much bigger than 10' x 20'. More than not wanting to get hurt or to hurt someone, I'm acutely aware that getting into a fight, even in self-defense, is going to result in a write-up, a loss of privileges, and worse a major setback to my timely release.

What would you do?!

I desperately try to avoid Adam's attacks so I can also, hopefully, avoid any backlash or setback for being involved in this commotion. I'm jumping over beds while he chases me screaming. I am able to slip out the door but he is right behind me. I yell, "Help! He's lost it!" Staff was already on the way. Even at this point nobody had so much as touched another. Nothing was broken and no one was hurt.

Regardless of the fact that I did nothing wrong, I am thrown in the hole and just lost everything I had been working so hard to obtain. Moreover, I get a write-up for assault. I'm not freaking out but can't believe this happened. I'm in the hole awaiting the outcome of the incident review which will determine how long I have to stay here. Both the Warden and the Chaplain visited me in the hole to figure out what happened and talk about solutions.

A good guy I know named James is next to me in the hole. He is always getting himself into trouble despite his good heart. He is another inmate that I was fortunate enough to help get his GED. We took classes together, walked laps, and studied law. While we are in the hole we are talking about Jesus. He asks if I want to see something cool that explains what the Bible really is. I, of course, say, "Absolutely!" He "fishes[25]" a piece of paper to me with the following acronym written on it:

Believers **I**nstructions **B**efore **L**eaving **E**arth.

This changed my view of what the Bible really is and these words helped me that day and still do today.

---

[25] Inmates use thin strings ripped from bedsheets to pass notes, and sometimes, drugs to other inmates in adjacent cells. This is considered an offense worthy of a write-up.

SECOND SHOT AT ALPHA

I am still in the hole in Kenai after the incident with Adam. The chaplain comes to talk with me. He tells me that they had a meeting and, "all of Alpha wants you to come back." I was excited to get back in there and get back on track. But, first, like anyone who gets a write-up, I had to go to a Disciplinary Board or, "D Board," to discuss my write-up and, hopefully, get it dropped. My cellie, Adam, that just lost it is lying and will not cop to what happened in the incident. However, the six other guys he threatened just two minutes prior to coming after me told the Chaplain what actually happened.

Then my cellie wrote me a letter stating he was in the wrong and had been jealous of me. So, as I prepare for my D Board I am organizing my defense: cellie's letter confessing to his behavior; statements from the six others verifying what actually happened; statement from the guy who wrote the message on the board confirming I told him to erase it. I was trying to do the right thing!

At the D Board hearing I present my evidence and confirm that, despite the ruckus, there was no physical contact by me or any verbal threats, other than me telling Adam to "STOP!" With the facts on my side, thankfully they dismissed all sanctions against me. So, I was released from the hole with no write-up. However, I was told I could not go back to Alpha. Strangely, Adam was allowed back in. I was sad but, once again, I didn't have a choice. I can

98

only guess that the Chaplain and the Warden figured Adam needed it more than I did. Nonetheless, I remained friends with the other Alpha members. They all wanted me back in the program and told me it was wrong that they wouldn't let me.

Despite my frustration I am still doing really well; about to enroll in college classes, faithfully doing my programming, and still working two jobs. I ask for my law librarian job back and get it the same day. So, now I have three jobs and I focus on helping more guys get their GEDs. I have no mental health holds and the only issue is this setback from the incident while I was hanging out with God more in Alpha. I'm still reading the Word and daily going to see the chaplain and having Bible studies.

Since I wasn't in Alpha any longer, I get transferred upstairs and off the program floor. I get put in a cell with a Native Alaskan and a white guy. I actually like both of them a lot. We get along great and the white guy is rowdy; tattooing, making home-made shanks, doing drugs. The Native is low-key and trying to do good.

It's tax season. Yeah, you gotta do them even in prison and I'm pretty good at doing them. So, I start doing them for other inmates. It's a fast and honest way to make money. They need the help and I actually have the capabilities to help. I actually get to do taxes for some of the guards as well. I'm trusted and everyone knows I am trying to do the right thing. From this point on I become the go-to guy for taxes in the prison.

However, there is a scam going on by the inmates and they're racking up hundreds of thousands of dollars right under the community's nose. The scam is basically they use stolen social security numbers to impersonate someone and fraudulently file taxes and direct the refund to a bank account they control and can access. The guys running the scam would coerce the weaker and/or newer inmates into participating in the scam and give them a small cut of the ill-gotten money. Some of the prison staff are even involved. Later in my incarceration I learn that one year there was about $750,000 ripped off from the government and unsuspecting citizens by inmates at one prison alone before officials found out and stopped it.

My cellies and I are missing write-ups by inches. That's how it is in prison; most guys do bad. Some try but even if you are doing good you are still dodging and weaving to avoid write-ups. If you do get one, the staff don't care but your family is disappointed in you. So, I am continually trying to stay write-up free.

One day I'm in our room with my white cellie and he shaves his head bald. This and his tattoos reveal that he is a racist and looks to be getting ready to join the KKK. I'm not into racism. Never have been. Plus, I like and get along with the black guys and the natives. He doesn't say anything to me about it but I find one of the KKK books and I'm super sad. My Native cellie sees the book as well. I tell him I'm not into this and am moving out. I write in for transfer and I'm moved to another room shortly thereafter.

Word travels fast in prison. The black guy, James, that I was in the hole with, heard that I had seen the book and moved rooms. He thanked me. I explained that it just isn't my thing. He took some of the programs I helped organize. He shook my hand and gave me a "bro" hug. I liked him.

CLASSIFICATION

During incarceration inmates are evaluated regularly. If the point of prison is to encourage rehabilitation and growth into a better member of society, then it makes sense that our progress is regularly monitored. So, classification hearings are held.

From the Alaska Department of Corrections policies[26]:

Classification: A process that systematically subdivides a prisoner population into groups based on custody and individual rehabilitative program needs.

1. Initial Classification: is the first classification of a prisoner which occurs within five (5) days of remand, and is used only once during incarceration.

2. Reclassification: is the classification of a *prisoner which occurs one year after the initial classification and annually thereafter as well as six months prior to release.*

Classification is super important to determining your life in prison. It affects your privileges related to being considered "Maximum" custody or "Medium" custody, which determines where you live and who you live with, etc.

---

[26] https://doc.alaska.gov/pnp/pdf/700.01.pdf

In September 2011 in Kenai I was at a Medium Custody level. I requested an interview to appeal my classification in an attempt to be lowered to Minimum Custody. See below:

I was arguing that my background and good behavior in prison should make me eligible to be moved down to Minimum Custody. This is the response I received:

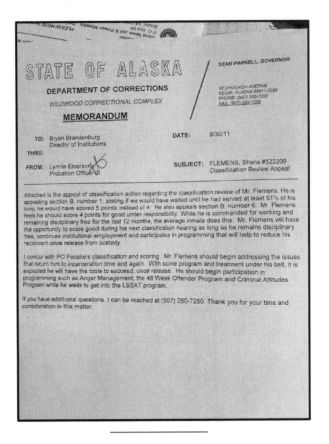

STATE OF ALASKA

SEAN PARNELL, GOVERNOR

DEPARTMENT OF CORRECTIONS

WILDWOOD CORRECTIONAL COMPLEX

10 CHUGACH AVENUE
KENAI, ALASKA 99611-7699
PHONE: (907) 260-7200
FAX: (907) 283-7308

MEMORANDUM

TO: Bryan Brandenburg Director of Institutions	**DATE:**	9/30/11
THRU:		
FROM: Lynnie Einerson Probation Officer II	**SUBJECT:**	FLEMENS, Shane #522209 Classification Review Appeal

Attached is the appeal of classification action regarding the classification review of Mr. Flemens. He is appealing section B, number 1; stating if we would have waited until he had served at least 51% of his time; he would have scored 5 points instead of 4. He also appeals section B, number 6. Mr. Flemens feels he should score 4 points for good under responsibility. While he is commended for working and remaining disciplinary free for the last 12 months, the average inmate does this. Mr. Flemens will have the opportunity to score good during his next classification hearing as long as he remains disciplinary free, continues institutional employment and participates in programming that will help to reduce his recidivism once release from custody.

I concur with PO Fenske's classification and scoring. Mr. Flemens should begin addressing the issues that return him to incarceration time and again. With some program and treatment under his belt, it is expected he will have the tools to succeed, once release. He should begin participation in programming such as Anger Management, the 48 Week Offender Program and Criminal Attitudes Program while he waits to get into the LSSAT program.

If you have additional questions, I can be reached at (907) 260-7250. Thank you for your time and consideration in this matter.

I am basically told that my classification will not be changing and am encouraged to "begin participation" in programming; "programming that will help to reduce his recidivism once release *[sic]* from custody." The thing is I already *am* in this programming, fully employed, and "disciplinary free." The PO writes that if I do these things that I will be able to "score good *[sic]*" in my next classification hearing.

While this would be great advice if I wasn't already doing all I could do it's really frustrating. But, as usual, I do my best to "accept the things I cannot change" and keep moving forward.

Fast forward seven months to my reclassification hearing in April 2012. I had done everything I was told to do in the response letter to my appeal and which I was already doing anyway. The result of this hearing was to deny my reclassification, so I stay at Medium level. But, perversely, *a week later* I am shipped back to Seward, a maximum-security facility.

This is an unfortunate example of how the system simply doesn't work and rarely seems to make sense. I am behaving well-enough to be moved to a Medium Custody level but not well enough to stay at a medium-security facility in Kenai?! I am being moved to a facility where 95%+ of the inmates have extreme behavioral issues and write-ups are the rule, not the exception. I am doing the programming designed to reduce my chances of recidivating but there seems to be no thought of the negative impact this move will have on me as my progress is interrupted and I am forced to basically start over in Seward.

QUESTION:

Why would you send a Medium Custody inmate (me) to a maximum-security prison (Seward)? What is the message being sent to inmates? What impact does a move like this have on actually reducing recidivism?

CERTIFICATE

I am in maximum-security at Seward now, months since my time in Kenai and the way that the Alpha situation went down is gnawing at my heart. I had worked really hard in the program and still can't believe that I got kicked out of it. Of all the programs I did in prison, and I did a ton of them, this was the one that impacted me the most. I decided I wanted, and felt like I deserved, my Alpha certificate. It's a big deal to get your certificate because it represents an important accomplishment. So, I appealed to the Program. I got an amazing letter from my wonderful mentor, John. It meant so much to me that he stood up for me and saw beyond the drama.

Thanks largely to John's letter, and backed-up by my friends in Alpha, my appeal was heard and I received this great news from the Chaplain, who we called "Chap." When I got this news I had already been shipped away to a medium-security prison in Colorado due to the overcrowding situation in Alaskan prisons, including Seward[27]. Getting this letter and certificate delivered to me there was a bright ray of sunshine.

Shane Flemens #522209
Hudson Correctional Facility
3001 N. Juniper St.
Hudson, Colorado 80642-9400

ALPHA

October 12, 2012

Greetings Shane:

I have received your appeal letter and attachments. After prayerful consideration and discussion with men who were in the program while you were resident, I grant your request.

John Evanson is a friend and brother in the Lord. I made a point to hear his perspective in your behalf.

Derek Ludington, who has returned to the program, spoke very favorably about you, and your being granted a Certificate.

I have enclosed a Certificate of Completion from the Alpha Re-Entry Initiative for you. Congratulations! I commend your manner in making this appeal. Keep the Faith, and go with God into your future. Proverb 27:17

Shalom

Stanley T. Wells
Director & Chaplain
Alpha Re-Entry Initiative
Wildwood Correctional Complex
10 Chugach Ave.
Kenai, Alaska 99611

Cc: John Evanson

Enc.

---

[27] http://www.sitnews.us/0610news/060410/060410_prisons.html

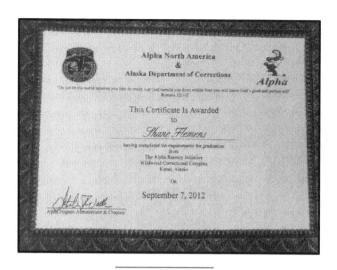

While getting my certificate felt really good, I was still sad to have been removed from a program where I was genuinely benefitting. I was contributing and helping guys make progress. It all still makes me just scratch my head and ask, "Is the system running as it should?" My answer all day long is, NO! But I am proud of my time in Alpha and am so grateful I was able to get my certificate.

THERE HAS TO BE A BETTER WAY

The more I have reflected on my time in prison and the many experiences I had personally, and the hundreds more I heard and witnessed, the more I have come to realize that the system is severely broken. If the point of prison is to help people like me, human beings like you, deal with their past mistakes we are failing as a society.

I have shared on these pages a raw and personal look into my journey through the correctional system in Alaska. There's nothing pretty or remotely easy about being in prison. It is truly the closest thing to hell on earth. You may think something like, "Hell on earth sounds about right. What else would motivate criminals to reform so they never have to go back." I actually understand that and you may have a point.

But here's the cold, hard truth about recidivism in Alaska:

In 2019, more than __6 out of 10__ offenders released from prison were re-incarcerated within __three__ years[28] And 2/3 of those offenders are re-incarcerated within 6 months!

Put another way, three years after being released from prison less than 40% of offenders manage to stay free. Alaska's recidivism rate is the 2nd highest in the nation, with Delaware being the worst.

---

[28] https://worldpopulationreview.com/state-rankings/recidivism-rates-by-state

If we are going to justly punish criminals who made someone else's life hell through their crimes, *and* encourage would-be prisoners to make better choices, then prison generally makes sense. But a 60%+ recidivism rate is nowhere close to anyone's definition of success.

We simply can't stop trying to find a better way to rehabilitate those individuals who will eventually be released *while* they are in prison. Without a system and process that works to actually "correct" problems and help offenders reform, then we, as a nation, will continue to waste billions and billions of taxpayer dollars and inflict this hell on our fellow citizens for really poor, if any, results. And, as I saw firsthand, so many of my fellow inmates were for years, and may still be, suffering from deep personal trauma, mental health issues, and personal struggles.

Further, we can never forget the families who also are and will be impacted by incarceration. Like my kids, too many kids grow up with a parent in prison. Like my mother, too many mothers worry themselves sick imagining what's happening to their child behind prison walls.

I am one man. I made big mistakes. I paid a price.

My strategy for managing my time in lock-up was simple: **I did my very best to do what I was told to do.** It worked for me. It didn't work perfectly but the more I let God into my life it worked even better. I have been out for five years now and will continue to do everything in my power to never go back to prison.

Please remember this quote by Nelson Mandela I shared at the start of this book:

"A nation should not be judged by how it treats its highest citizens, but its lowest ones."

It is hard to imagine a "lower citizen" than a locked-up prisoner. As you have read, life in prison is base, raw, dangerous, sad, and often terrifying. The 2020 budget for the Department of Corrections for the State of Alaska is $380MM[29].

I have asked questions throughout the book to get you to think about the purpose of prison and the enormous amounts of money our nation spends on trying to protect our communities from violence and crime. I hope you have seen, at least a little, that locking up criminals and forgetting about them won't work. Remember that for the 6 out of 10 offenders that are released and then return to an Alaskan prison within three years of release, there is at least one member of the community who was a victim of their crime. This is a cycle that we have to stop.

I have one last question. OK, well, three questions:

---

[29] https://omb.alaska.gov/html/performance/program-indicators.html?p=24&r=1

QUESTIONS:

Do you think it's acceptable to spend almost $400MM per year in Alaska only to have 6 out of 10 released inmates commit crime again and be re-incarcerated within three years?

Do you think that the policies and treatment like I faced in prison are helpful or harmful to keeping inmates from recidivating, i.e. going back to prison?

Is it possible that this high rate of recidivism, which costs taxpayers billions of dollars a year and untold non-financial costs to families and communities, is partially caused by the system itself and the people running it? If so, why would that be?

AFTERWORD

Thank you for taking the time to read my book. It means a lot to me and I am very grateful.

My next book (#3) is already in the works. I will, of course, share even more stories and lessons from my time inside and take a hard look at solutions to move the criminal justice system from one of punishment to progress; towards real growth.

Please make good choices. Be kind. Be good. Let God lead you. He will bless you more than you know.

ABOUT THE AUTHOR

Since his release from prison in 2015, Shane Flemens of Wenatchee, Washington has been successfully running his own landscaping and general contracting company, ABE Landscaping and Maintenance. He also owns and operates Rise n' Ride Rentals, a watersport company with his daughter, Ashley.

He is passionate about transforming yards into beautiful retreats where people can spend their most valuable asset—time, with their families and friends.

Now a free man, Shane is driven to shine a bright light on the darkness of prison through his writings, which he began on the inside: ask hard questions and share truth. He hopes that through these stories, and those of his fellow inmates, he can affect positive change in the lives of others.

His three grandchildren, Lilly, Amaya, and Mateo, are the light of his world.

Made in the USA
Columbia, SC
17 January 2024

29754643R00069